# ARE YOU READY TO RETIRE?

## *The Non-financial Side of Retirement*

*by*
*Don Curtis*

# Contents

# Are you psychologically ready to retire?

## Introduction

Retirement...Does it bring a vision of freedom from the daily grind, or fear of too much time on your hands? Does it bring the joy of new adventures and the time to pursue the things that you always wanted to do? Or does it bring deep depression and a loss of identity?

Every single day, 500 Canadians retire. In the following year and every year after that, they will have an additional 2,000 hours of free time. Some will have the time of their lives...some will go back to work...some will feel depressed. About 30% will have a real problem adjusting, while others will literally die of boredom.

2,000 extra hours per year!

If you are like most Canadians, you will enter this new and potentially long period of your life with no clear picture of what life will be like and no plan to make it successful and fulfilling.

But, as you will learn, those who approach retirement with a positive attitude and a plan of action can have the time of their lives. Why not be one of them?

# Notes

# *Retire from work, not life.*

## Chapter 1
## Getting There

Have you noticed that there are hundreds of books on the subject of the financial aspects of retirement? Plus, there are countless articles in magazines and newspapers about RRSP's, RIF's, GIC's, etc. And over $100,000,000 is spent annually on advertising at RRSP time in Canada.

However, there is almost nothing written about how to live successfully in retirement or how to mentally prepare for this major adjustment in your life -- not to mention the life of your spouse. Why is there such a dearth of information?

Several years ago, I started to research the topic and found little information. After much searching -- about five years worth in total -- I compiled the following text which I think the reader will find informative, eye-opening and rather fun as you get ready to be a successful retiree.  In the next few chapters, I will show you that retirement can be the greatest time of your life, a whole new chance to do the things you always wanted to do but never had the time.  Retirement gives you that gift of time.

## *Life begins at retirement.*

Have you thought about the dynamic changes in your life and lifestyle?

Have you thought about where you will live?

Does your spouse agree?

What are you going to do to fill in the time, to replace social contacts, routine and your "work" identity?

How will you replace the satisfaction and sense of accomplishment that you derived from work?

How do you intend to live in and enjoy your retirement years?

Who are you?  And who are you going to be?

## *Are You Ready to Retire?*

# Do you have a plan?

If you are like most Canadians approaching retirement, you probably do not have a plan. Why not?

You have a plan for the financial side of retirement (or you had better!).  Did you know that only about 60% of working Canadians contribute regularly to an RRSP? And that the average annual contribution is only $4700?  In 2010, only 26% of eligible taxpayers made any contribution ($34 billion out of a potential $717 billion) with the average total accumulation being only $40,000.  It is not enough.  Who do they think is going to look after them in their old age? Their kids?  The government?  If you listen closely, you will hear the sound of laughter. Wake up!

The only person who is going to look after you in your old age is you.  It is your responsibility to plan for your retirement, both financially and non-financially.  With the number of Canadians who have a life retirement plan being almost nil, it's a good job that you are reading this book.

In <u>Money and the Meaning of Life</u> by Jacob Needleman, the author points out that there is nothing inherent in money that makes us happy.  Money has nothing to do with Wealth of Experience, Wealth of Knowledge, Wealth of True Friends, nor Wealth of Creativity.  To have any and all of these is to be truly wealthy.

# Aging

First, the bad news:  You are getting older!  I tell you that because aging seems to be one of the most unexpected events in life.  Now the good news:  The entire concept of aging has dramatically changed over the last couple of generations.  According to Ken Dychtwald in his book Age Wave, just two generations ago, *"65 was old.  It was time to quit.  Time to act your age.  Time to sleep and play Mah-jong.  The greatest moments of your life were gone and you could expect no more.  You were out to pasture."*

Ken calls this gerontophobia, and its mantra is, *"If young is good, old is bad; if young is creative and dynamic, old must be dull and staid; if young is beautiful, then old must be unattractive; if young is exciting, old must be boring; if young is full of passion, old must be beyond passion."*

Fortunately, for those about to reach retirement age, this is no longer the case. In the 1700's, life expectancy in North America was 35 years. One hundred years later, it had only risen to 40. In fact, throughout recorded history, only 1 in 10 people ever lived to 65! Today, over 80% do -- and currently, over 20% of baby boomers will be 65, and by 2020, all of them will have reached this milestone. As Age Wave points out, *"We are facing a revolution of which there is no precedent in history."*

This dramatic increase in life expectancy is not the result of some magic elixir. It is the logical result of better food, better diet, better health care, and regular exercise. Did you know that study after study shows that regular exercise is the single most important factor in sustaining good health? It is the closest thing we have to the Fountain of Youth. And guess who has the time to exercise now?

In their book, <u>Successful Aging</u>, Kahn and Rowe detail the findings of a ten-year, $10 million study on aging, and they came to a simple conclusion: *"We are in large part responsible for our own old age. Because being overweight, out of shape and hypertensive, as well as having high cholesterol and high triglycerides are not, for the most part, inherited. They are a function of how we choose to live."*

Canadian men retiring today can expect to live another 23.3 years; women another 28.2 years. Therefore, time is on your side.

## *Old age is 15 years older than I am.*

You are going to be retired for a very long time and, as such, you might as well make the most of it. And you might as well be good at it.

A summary of what we have learned in Chapter 1:

1.  Plan ahead.  No plan is a plan to fail.
2.  You are getting older, but not necessarily old.
3.  And you are going to be retired for a very long time.

# Chapter 2
# Retirement at 65?

Did you ever stop and think where the heck the concept of retiring at 65 came from? Well, it actually started with Chancellor Otto Von Bismarck of Prussia, who introduced the first social security in 1887. He chose the biblical three score and ten, but the number was later reduced to 65 by his government.

But before you congratulate old Otto on his benevolence, let me state that life expectancy in Prussia at that time was a mere 45! Using the same math today would mean you would not receive your first social security cheque until 20 years after you died. For interest, the Canadian government incorporated a retirement age of 65 in the 1920's, when life expectancy was 61, therefore being only slightly more benevolent than Otto. But cheer up! In 1876, 80% of mean in North America over 65 still worked. Now, 15% do.

As noted, the generation that is about to retire will conceivably spend one-third of their lives being retired.  That's a long time to fill in, or it can be the greatest opportunity you are ever going to have to do all of the things you always wanted to.  The choice is entirely yours to make.  For the remainder of this book -- in fact, for the remainder of your life -- I want you to keep this simple hypothesis in mind.

> Why in the world would you want to prolong work or despair at its ending, when there are so many wonderful and wondrous things that you can do with your energy, your talents, and your creativity?

# Work: What's it All About?

Of interest, let's briefly examine the subject of work. What's so great about it, that so many people miss it when it's gone?

To be fair, here's the good list:

- money
- social contacts
- sense of achievement
- sense of contribution to your family and society
- self-definition
- self-fulfillment

Now for the bad list:

- staying inside on a sunny day
- recycled air
- rush-hour traffic...twice!
- your boss
- incompetent co-workers

- office politics
- no time
- overtime
- stressssssssssssssssssssssssssssssss

Doesn't sound like work should be too terribly hard to give up.  Read the list again. Why do people replace the stress of working with the stress of not working?  Why do they feel guilty about not working, or feel guilty about having more fun?  Who's to blame for this backward thinking?

If we go back to ancient Rome or Greece, work was for the uneducated, for the unenlightened.  Those who were enlightened preferred to spend their time contemplating the finer things in life:  arts, culture, and knowledge.  The Greek word for leisure is *skhole*, from which we derive the word school.  If we could tell these civilizations that people in the future would feel guilty about not working, they would think us dazed.  So what changed?

Two things: The Industrial Revolution and the Protestant Work Ethic.

The Industrial Revolution changed the world from an agrarian society to an industrial one. This necessitated work in cities. Then wages, bills and, of course, taxes.

The Protestant Work Ethic told us that work was good. You know, "Keep your nose to the grindstone and your shoulder to the wheel. Put in a good day's work, by the sweat of your brow." If work was good, then leisure must be bad, slothful and unproductive. Leisure, if you had any, was only a short rest so you could work harder; it was not an end unto itself. And you bought it -- hook, line and sinker. Yes, you did!

So here is a brief Retirement Test....

Have you ever felt guilty about being on vacation?
Do you ever brag about how busy you are?
Do you regularly take work home?

Do you take your laptop on vacation?
Have you missed an important family event because of work?
In the words of Tennessee Ernie Ford, *"Do you owe your soul to the company store?"*

If you answered yes to three or more of the above, shame on you!  You are a lousy candidate for a successful retirement and it is a good job you are reading this book.

Before we continue, I should point out that I am not really against work.  It's what you do from age 20 to 65, and it is a necessary and valuable part of life's journey -- not the least of which is to give you the financial means to raise a family, build a career and give purpose to your life.

# The Time Crunch

Mahatma Ghandi said, *"There is more to life than increasing its speed."*

Yet, that is exactly what we have been doing. And Alabama, the country singing group, captured this lunacy in their hit song which lamented,

> *"I'm in a hurry to get things done*
> *I rush and rush until life's no fun*
> *All I do is live and die*
> *I'm in a hurry and don't know why."*

As an aside, did you ever think that you would see quotes by Ghandi and Alabama in the same context?

# Stress

Lack of time leads to stress and the price is enormous. Heart disease has increased by 500% in the last 50 years. Millions of people suffer from high blood pressure and, believe it or not, our neighbours to the south consume 16 tons of aspirin every year.

If a lot of stress is caused by a lack of time, then the really good news for those about to retire (or have already done so) is that you have lots of time to do whatever you want. You should have less stress and less worry. As Alfred E. Newman of Mad Magazine says, *"What, me worry?"* Alfred is right.

Did you know that 44% of things you worry about never happen? 30% have already happened and there is nothing you can do about them. 22% are completely trivial. That's 96%. So you are causing yourself all that worry and stress for nothing...okay, for 4%. In fact, 43% of retirees report that with less stress and more time to exercise, their health improved after retirement.

A summary of what we have learned in Chapter 2:

1. Time is on your side.
2. You are going to be retired for a long time.
3. What's so great about work that you would miss it when it's over?
4. There is a whole world of wonderful things waiting for you to explore, and now you have the time to pursue them. Lucky you!
5. Don't replace the stress of working with the stress of not working.

---

Did you know that it takes 3 weeks to break a habit, 6 weeks to make a habit, and 36 weeks to hotwire it into your brain?

---

# Chapter 3
# Who Are You?

> The day you retire is the day you find out who you really are.

Having just discussed the stress of having no time in our lives, how odd is it that so many people have trouble with having lots of time?

The world is filled with people bemoaning the fact that they have no time to enjoy life, to play, to read, to think.

But retirement is going to give you the gift of time. And it's free! You have quite a responsibility not to squander it.

I mentioned in Chapter 1 that there was very little written about the mental side of retirement, and there seems to be a lack of research on the subject as well. This, despite the fact that baby boomers are fast approaching retirement age and will wield enormous political and financial clout.

I did, however, come across a study conducted right here in Ontario.  It is detailed n a book by Morris M. Schnore entitled, Retirement, Bane or Blessing?  The study explored attitudes toward retirement among 750 men and women, both working and retired.  The study found that positive attitudes and negative attitudes to retirement are a huge determinant on the nature of your adjustment to being retired.  Those who are happy in retirement:

• had a high level of satisfaction with their standard of living
• had a positive attitude to their health
• were satisfied with what they had
• believed that the best things in life were free
• believed that they were better off than most.

The group of successful retirees also believed that they controlled what happened to them. They had devalued the need to accumulate the outward signs of status.  They are, in fact, the bulk of retirees.

For those in the study who held negative views of retirement, it should come as no surprise that work held a central part in their lives.  It was and is the very definition of who and what they are.

Plato:  *"He who is of a calm and happy nature will hardly feel the presence of age.  But to him who is of the opposite disposition, youth and age are equally a burden."*

Another study (1990), this one by the Marriott Corporation, discovered that 50% of those over 65 felt that they were living the best years of their lives.  Clearly one of the key secrets of successful retirement is a positive attitude.  Not surprisingly, many of these successful retirees had a plan of action. They didn't stumble into retirement.  Just as it is true that the sooner you start your RRSP, the better off you will be.  The sooner you start your Retirement Action Plan, the more rewarding it will be as well.  Maybe we should call it **The Registered Retirement Life Plan** or **RRLP**.

Who are you?  Really?

Have you thought about it?  If you are John the architect or Christine the accountant, and that's all you are in your mind, then you are going to have trouble being retired.  Too many of us define ourselves by what we do at work.  Our job has become our self-definition and because of that, our sole source of self-esteem.  We are consumed with doing, not being.  We take meaning only from what we do, not what we are.  And our cell phones, pagers, text messaging only add to this problem.  Take away the job and what is left?  This is the number one cause of retirement depression and failure…"I don't know who I am anymore.  I'm nobody, I have no self-worth to society and no worth to myself."

> The question is not so much what happens to people when they retire, but what happens in people.

Many people who hold positions of authority lead dual lives. One life is lived in business – a world of competition, striving, power, and achievement. The other is life lived in the smaller world of home, family, marriage and children. It is, in fact, into this smaller world we retreat when the pressures of the other grows too strong.

And the balance of shifting from one to the other often determines one's emotional stability. When we retire, this smaller world becomes the permanent exile from the world in which we spent the bulk of our lives. This emotional and physical shift can cause severe consequences in your life...and on the person who has been occupying that space all along: your spouse.

Being stripped of all authority triggers anxiety. All of a sudden, we have reached the place where our work history ends. We can now clearly measure the entire distance from where we started, to the farthest point we are ever going to get in our work lives. Maybe you dreamed of becoming president of your company or reaching a certain salary or being recognized for a major achievement, and you didn't quite make it. I emphasize this point because retirement is very difficult for these people. In their minds, the whistle has blown and the game is over.

But I can tell you that it is only one game. You have a whole different life ahead of you in which to set and achieve new goals!

This is all the more reason to have a plan of action. To set new goals and to put a process in place to find, identify and enjoy a new game.

(Case in point...Twelve years after I retired, I launched a history website that in only 90 days reached over 1,000,000 views worldwide and was declared by Google/YouTube as the fastest growing history website in the world!)

I am reminded of a television show I saw some years ago.  It showed people in an old age home staring blankly out the window, simply waiting for death to call.  This was contrasted with the morning run of a men's jogging club, the youngest member of which was 80.  And a 96-year-old movie director, full of life, about to shoot a new movie and who had two others in the works.  The message was very clear -- activity and interests prolong life and its enjoyment.

> Retirement means no stress and no anxiety unless, of course, you play golf.

A summary of what we have learned in Chapter 3:

1. Your attitude to retirement is critical to its success.
2. Who are you?  You are about to find out.
3. The game is not over, it's just a new game. Learn to play it well.

# Chapter 4
## Social Contacts, Purpose and Routine

Work, or more correctly, the workplace, provides three key elements that most people require in their lives:

1.  Social contacts -- people we see and interact with on a daily basis and who share the same corporate goals.
2.  Purpose in what we are doing.
3.  Routine – I get up at 7:00, go to work at 8:00, etc.

Studies have shown that when we lose these three basic needs, we feel lost, alone, and at loose ends.  Therefore, it is critical to replace all three in retirement.  ASAP.

## People/Contacts

Work is certainly not the only place to find regular social contacts.  There are numerous clubs, groups, and organizations in your community (Rotary, Kiwanis, Masons, etc.) and a host of hobby groups, sports groups, craft groups, etc.  And don't forget volunteer organizations!

And, of course, you can keep old relationships alive.  Take the responsibility of maintaining them -- the rewards are worth it.

## Purpose

You will also need to decide what your new purposes in life are going to be.  I purposely used the plural, because you can have several now that you have all this extra time!  Be the best grandfather in the world, or the best friend, or the best volunteer.  But whatever, be the best retired person you know.  Think about it, decide what you will do and then pursue it with vigour.

Remember that boredom is a waste of time.  It is insidious.  It can lead to stress, headaches, backaches and insomnia.  The best way to fight boredom is to find something that you like to do and embrace it for all it is worth.  There are hundreds of things to do, regardless of age.  And I should mention here that being alone does not have to mean being lonely.  Solitude -- enjoying a quite moment by yourself -- is very rewarding.  Read a book, walk in the woods, watch a sunset.  Remember all the times at work when you wished for a moment's peace?  Well, lucky you!  Here they are...free for the taking.

The difference between being lonely and being alone is only a matter of perspective.

# Routine

You will need to establish a daily or weekly routine.  Get up at a specific time each day. Exercise for one hour, go for a morning walk, go to the gym, meet friends on a specific day, play golf, go boating, ride your bike, join a club, pursue your hobbies in a more organized manor.  This is all part of your plan of action.  Avoid at all cost getting up with nothing to do on any given day.

## Is Your Spouse Ready to Retire?

> When a man retires, his wife gets twice the man and half the income.

Speaking of not being alone, perhaps this is a good time to talk about your spouse.  The topic of the discussion is, *Are You Ready to*

*Retire?*  But is your spouse ready to have you retire, ready to have you invade her space? Remember that she already has contacts, purpose and routine associated with her place, and you are about to disturb that balance.  This can result in friction.  After all, she married you for better or for worse, but not for lunch every single day!

Perhaps you dreamed of retirement in the country or on a boat, but your spouse has no intention of doing either.  Problem!  As part of your action plan, you both need to sit down well in advance of retiring and talk about these issues.  Find common ground and decide what you will do together and alone, where you will live, etc.

Now that you have explored the replacement of people, purpose and routine, as well as making some important decisions in concert with your spouse, it is time to focus on what you are going to do to fill your extra 2,000 hours each year.

As a famous advertisement once said, *"I always wanted to learn to play the piano, but they said it would take ten years.  Of course, that was ten years ago!"*  Tsk, tsk.  Wouldn't it be the absolute worst thing in the world to reach the end of life and not really have tried to do what you really wanted to do?

Retirees!  This is your chance!  Your time has come!

Ralph Waldo Emerson wrote, *"We are always getting ready to live, but not really doing it."*  According to Dr. Layne Longfellow, a professor of psychology who lectures on stress management, *"Most of us walk around believing that any day now life will stop being difficult, stop throwing those annoying little surprises at us, and then all will be fine.  But life just doesn't work that way."*

A summary of what we have learned in Chapter 4:

1.  You must replace the social contacts, purpose and routine of work.
2.  Make sure that you and your spouse are on the same page when it comes to retirement plans.

# Chapter 5
# Developing Your Plan

> How old would you be if you didn't know
> how old you were?

Earlier, we examined all the wonderful and wondrous things you could do with your newfound and well-deserved time. Well, the time has come to decide on some of those things!

From now on, I want you to start thinking of retirement as your new career, and I want you to be really good at it.

Take a few minutes, and write down all the things that you always wanted to do if you had the time. They might be things that you do now, but would like to do better. They might be things that you always intended to do, but never got around to doing. Or they might be things that you did years ago, but gave up for more pressing obligations. Or maybe they are things that you never thought of before, but now challenge you creatively, mentally or physically. See if you can get 50 ideas in the spaces below.

1.  Things that you already do but would like to do more often and better.

      _____

      _____

      _____

      _____

      _____

      _____

      _____

      _____

      _____

      _____

      _____

2.  Things that you always intended to do
    but never had the time.

    _____

    _____

    _____

    _____

    _____

    _____

    _____

    _____

    _____

    _____

3.  Things that you did years ago and gave
    up because of other commitments.

    _____

    _____

    _____

    _____

_____

_____

_____

_____

_____

_____

_____

_____

_____

4.  Things that you never thought of doing
    before but which are now of interest.

_____

_____

_____

_____

_____

_____

_____

_____

_____

_____

_____

_____

Now, pick the top five and then get started!

Congratulations!  You are well on your way to a successful retirement.  If you want to explore ideas more deeply, I highly recommend a terrific book by Ernie J. Zelinski, <u>The Joy of Not Working</u>.

Just to stimulate your list, here is mine (I have marked the ones I have done in **Bold**, so I still have many to go!):

**walk**, bike, **horseback ride, learn Tai Chi, read in a library, read more books, kayak**, swim, dance, **dine out once a week**, go to lectures, **give lectures**, go on a dinosaur dig, **go on a cattle drive**, visit museums and art galleries, paint, write letters, **write articles, write books (like this one!), research the family**

**tree**, **study history**, travel back roads, **ride a reining horse**, ride a cutting horse, sail, **make things out of wood**, **collect antiques**, **trap shoot**, go to local baseball games, master the computer, go to concerts, **use my skills to help the community and charities**

A word of advice:  Don't think that you can retire on Friday and take up 5 new activities on Monday!  Don't try to shift from all work to all leisure.  It's too hard.  You will have a much easier time if you start a few of the activities well before you retire.  These will help your new self-definition and establish new regular contacts, purpose and routine.  And you will be more proficient at them by the time you retire.

The more on-going interests you have, the easier the transition.  In fact, the pursuit of these new activities will very much start to forge your new self-definition.  The best self-definition will be derived from the things that you are most passionate about pursuing...the things that others will associate with your true essence.

Take a look at your list and decide which things you will do on your own, and which you will share with your spouse, old friends, and new friends.  The best choices will be a balance.  And the choices will determine the people you meet, your level of exercise and your level of satisfaction.

Regardless of choice, the secret of success is to plan now and get started...NOW!

## Living the Moment

Most people are very bad at this task.  We are always too busy worrying about the future to notice the now.  And if you miss the now, you miss the magic moments.  Moments you can never get back.

Horace Mann wrote, *"Lost yesterday, somewhere between sunrise and sunset, two golden moments.  No reward is offered, for they are gone forever."*

You need to do whatever you are doing to the fullest, no matter how simple or trivial.  Don't rush.  Train yourself to recognize and enjoy the hundreds of moments that you will encounter.  Take a moment when someone needs a friend, take a moment with a child to really look at a fluffy dandelion, stop and pet a dog in the park, park on a country road and smell the air, walk through a cornfield, enjoy a sunset and a sunrise, marvel at the colour of the sky, go on a trip and actually get to know someone who lives there.

My favourite character from a movie is Augustus McCrae, in "Lonesome Dove", as played by Robert Duvall.  Augustus is a retired Texas Ranger who loves life and who lives for the moments.  I have watched this six-hour miniseries many times, and love the character because he has found the magic in everyday life.  In fact, Augustus believes that because his friend doesn't get enough fun out of life, it is up to him to get more to balance it.  How wonderful!

There was also a Lexus car commercial on air in 2006 that spoke to *moments*.  I wish I knew who wrote it so I could tell him how brilliant it is.  I boldly added to this text and with the unknown writer's indulgence.  I present it here:

A moment.

A moment, if you please.  Moments can be short, moments can be long.  There are moments of joy, moments of sorrow, moments of passion, moments that you will never forget, moments you've already forgotten, and moments you don't get.

There are awkward moments and moments of truth. "Hey, wait a moment!" "I need a moment." "You got a moment?" And, of course, you can leave on a moment's notice.

You can take a moment, make a moment, spoil a moment, seize a moment, share a moment, cherish a moment... And, if all the stars align at the right moment, that moment can be perfect.

Moments can define you, moments can delight you, and moments can change your life. You can live for the moment and, if you are really lucky, you can live in the moment -- even have a lifetime of moments, one after the other.

So here's to the moments, and squeezing all you can from every single one of them. Pursue *your moments for all they are worth, because they are worth a lot.*

I hope by now that you are beginning to see that you have an enormous gift coming your way. Having the time to pursue your passions will allow you to connect with your past, appreciate your now, and make the most out of your future.

A summary of what we have learned in Chapter 5:

1. Retirement is your new career.
2. Make a list of all the things you want to do. Start five. Now.
3. Learn to recognize and live in the moments.

# Chapter 6
# Nine Rules for a Successful Retirement

Now is not the time in your life to utter phrases such as:

"I can't do that."

or

"I'm too old to try."

Many people fall into this trap, thinking it is easier to cling to old beliefs and routines, rather than trying something new for fear of failure.  Well, get over it.

Take some risks.  Chances are that most of the things you gained in life were worth taking some risk to attain.  And besides, you're retired.  What should you care what someone else thinks, anyway!  What are they going to do -- fire you?  As Nike says, *"Just do it."*

Listed below are some of the secrets of a successful retirement, some of which we have explored in depth in the foregoing chapters. But it is worth reviewing them again, and adding a few more.  Read them carefully, for they can change your life.

# 1

Attitude -- a positive attitude to retirement is essential to its success.

# 2

Place -- the choices you make as to where to live in retirement impact who your friends will be, how much time you spend with family, and what range of activities are available to you.  Remember that you don't have to drive to work and, therefore, the choice of where you can live is endless. Location.  Location.  Location.

# 3

Take some risks with new ventures. If something is worth having, it is usually worth the effort to obtain it.

# 4

Resolve to take action. Having your list of planned activities is one thing. Acting on them is another. Try, explore, and experience.

# 5

Find out who you really are. It is critical to replace your work self-definition with your new self-definition. Maslow's Hierarchy of Needs places self-actualization as the highest level. He called this level the ultimate goal of human existence -- the most profound reason to live. Ken Dychtwald in Age Wave touched on this point as well; he categorized life in three phases:

i)   Up to age 25 -- time for the biological growth, learning and the development of personality.
ii)  Up to 60 -- a time of work, family and partnering.
iii) After 60 years of age -- the development of the interior self, a sense of self-actualization and sharing with others the lessons and experiences of life.

# 6

Cultivate friendships:  Having close personal friends is extremely important:  spouse, children, old and new friends.

# 7

Make healthy choices.  Your health is in your hands.  What you do with it is up to you.  I am reminded of George Burns' joke, *"If I knew I was going to live this long, I would have taken better care of myself."*

Unfortunately, the number one activity in North America is watching television and video screens. And these go hand in hand with overeating, a combination that has led to a frightening level of diabetes. While you are contemplating your health, think about these facts:

i)   Giving up smoking will add 2-9 years to your life.
ii)  Giving up heavy drinking will add 3-11 years to your life.
iii) Not being overweight can add 1-3 years to your life.
iv)  Regular exercise can add 1-2 years to your life.
v)   Reducing stress can add 1-5 years to your life.

This adds up to 8-30 years, so not only is your life your hands, but the length of that life as well!

# 8

Be creative with your choices.  Creativity is the full expression of your human spirit and it is to be cherished, nurtured and cultivated.  It is probably fair to say that to have a successful retirement, you have to be creative.  Someone just said, "But I'm not creative."  Hogwash!  I'll bet as a child, you were creative.  So be childish again.  Creativity is the best evidence of the child in all of us.  By being creative, you can design your new life rather than just survive it.

Creativity leads to ideas, ideas to action, and action to satisfaction.  Creativity takes place in the moments and, as we already know, you have to learn to live in the moments as they occur.  Creativity is the extra 10%.  It can overcome boredom, enrich your life, and arm you against the common.  It can make an ordinary day extraordinary.  Open up your imagination.  Take a chance.

# 9

Make a difference.  Ask yourself if in your job you made a difference to someone's life.  If so, good for you!  If not, now you have the time to accomplish this very noble and rewarding task.  Make a difference to someone, to your community, to the environment, etc.  By making a difference in someone else's life, you will make a huge difference in your own.  Albert Schweitzer said, *"The purpose of life is to serve and to share compassion and the will with others. Only then can we ourselves be human beings."*


A summary of what we have learned in Chapter 6:

1.  Take action.
2.  Make new friends.
3.  Make healthy choices.
4.  Be creative.
5.  Make a difference.

# Summary

1.  You are going to get older, and you presumably are going to retire. Don't let either sneak up on you.
2.  Get ready. Have a plan because you are going to be retired for a long time.
3.  Remember that leisure is good. And a lot of work was dumb anyway.
4.  Worry is also dumb. So is boredom *aka boredumb*.
5.  Type A personalities are wrong, despite the fact that they are dying to prove their point.
6.  Replace the people, purpose and routine of work with new people, new purposes, and new routines.
7.  Constantly add to your list of things to do and explore.
8.  Take action. As Buddha tells us, *"To know and not do, is not to know."*
9.  Take risks.
10. Learn. Laugh. Lighten up.
11. Be spontaneous.

12. Savour the moments.
13. You <u>can</u> teach an old dog new tricks.
14. Be creative everyday.
15. Make a difference in someone's life.
16. Cultivate new friends, new interests, and new passions.
17. Commit a random act of kindness.
18. Value yourself and the world will value you.
19. You are responsible for your own well-being...but also for your own boredom and worries.  Solve your own problems -- self-pity and bitterness will make you old before your time.
20. Exercise.
21. It is within your power to constantly change, adapt, and keep pace with life.
22. Open your mind, because a mind is like a parachute:  it works better when it is open.
23. Try and recapture the elation you had as a child when you mastered something for the first time.
24. Make successful retirement your new career and be really good at it.

25. Don't squander the best years of your life. They can be filled with wonderful new adventures. Look forward to the future and grab onto it for all it is worth.

26. Let's close with a quote from a lady named Nadine Star who, at age 85, wrote the following:

If I had my life to live over, I'd make more mistakes next time. I'd relax. I would limber up. I would be sillier than I have been on this trip. I would take fewer things seriously. I would take more chances. I would climb more mountains and swim more rivers. I would eat more ice cream and less beans. I would perhaps have more actual troubles, but I'd have fewer imaginary ones.

You see, I'm one of those people who live sensibly and sanely, hour after hour, day after day. Oh, I've had my moments, and if I had to do it over again, I'd have more of them. In fact, I'd try to have nothing else. Just moments, one after another, instead of living so many years ahead of each day. I've been one of those persons who never goes anywhere without a thermometer, a hot water bottle, and a raincoat. If I had to do it over again, I would travel lighter than I have.

If I had my life to live over, I would start barefoot earlier in the spring and stay that way later in the fall. I would go to more dances. I would ride more merry-go-rounds and I would pick more daisies!

# References, Books, Articles

- The Golden Revolution:  Retirement Styles for the 1990's by Jan Drabek
- The Joy of Not Working by Ernie J. Zelinski
- How to Retire Happy, Wild, and Free by Ernie J. Zelinski
- Closing Doors, Opening Worlds by Vern Drilling
- Age Wave by Ken Dychtwald
- Retirement:  Bane or Blessing? by Morris M. Schnore
- Working Ourselves to Death by Diane Fassel
- Solitude:  A Return to the Self by Anthony Storr
- Are You Happy? by Dennis Wholey
- The Time Bind by Arlie Russell Hochschild
- Poor Richard's Principle:  Recovering the American Dream by Robert Wuthnow

- Aging in Canada:  Social Perspectives by Victor W. Marshall
- Money and the Meaning of Life by Jacob Needleman
- Getting Unstuck by Dr. Sidney B. Simon
- Your Renaissance Years:  Making Retirement the Best Years of Your Life by Robert L. Veninga
- Shifting Gears to Your Life & Work After Retirement by Carolee Duckworth and Marie Langworthy
- Put Work in its Place by Bruce O'Hara
- Life Begins at Sixty by Bill Case
- Sixty Plus:  Planning It, Living It, Loving It by Allan Fromme
- The Reality of Retirement by Jules Z. Willing
- Secrets of Becoming a Late Bloomer: Staying Creative, Aware, and Involved in Midlife and Beyond by Connie Goldman and Richard Mahler

A few thoughts to leave you laughing…

In retirement, the spouse gets twice the husband and half the salary.

Denial is not a retirement plan.

It's not only the scenery you miss by going fast.

Don't think of it as retiring **from** something but, rather, **to** something.

Try to have a vocation vacation.

You can't turn back time, but you can rewind your clock now and then.

Henry Ford said, *"If you think you are right or you think that you are wrong, you are correct on both thoughts."*

Here is a sure-fire cure for boredom: do something!

Don't have any regrets when you die.

If you go around thinking that any day you may die, one of these days you will be correct.

There is no dress rehearsal for life, so get in the game, get on the stage, join the parade.

New friends and new adventures will not beat a path to YOUR door.

George Burns said that he was going to stay in showbiz until he was the only one left. He also said that every morning when he got up, he read the obituaries in the paper and if he didn't see his name he carried on. George vowed to play the London Palladium at 100 -- he almost made it.

Don Curtis is a marketing/advertising professional, and spent many years writing numerous bank and financial institution retirement product advertisements and brochures. In the mid-1990's, Don thought it would be a good idea for one of his clients to offer its customers advice on the non-financial side of retirement -- the psychological side. To his amazement, there was virtually nothing written on the subject. And so began a five-year quest to track down information and to study the problem and the need. The result is this book, a down-to-earth informative look at how to retire successfully. The book is chock full of sound advice and a must-read for anyone contemplating retirement in the next few years.